D1603801

Village of Knives

Helli Fang

INDEPENDENTLY PUBLISHED BY
DRIFTWOOD PRESS

Independently published by Driftwood Press
in the United States of America.

Managing Poetry Editor: Jerrod Schwarz
Cover Image: Sam Alden
Cover Design: Sally Franckowiak
Innards Design & Copyeditor: James McNulty
Fonts: Existence, Centaur, Garamond, Adobe Ming Std,
Times New Roman, & Merriweather

First published in February 2020
ISBN-13: 978-1-949065-06-0

Please visit our website at www.driftwoodpress.net
or email us at editor@driftwoodpress.net.

Contents

ars poetica

caged in the herring's rib, my throat,
bleached blue by silence, pulled
the last latch, limbs still

strapped to a bullet
belonging to someone else: &
when my body entered flesh

it turned into rain, an arrowhead
boxcut from stalactite
and salt, trying to spin a bowl

of wedding rings back
into clay, miming a language
with ice cubes for teeth: not about

where the lake hides, but whether
it wants to be seen. to write a poem
is to build a burning body.

Genesis

What do you call it	when a man swallows smoke
	& you never see it exit him
What do you call it	when you wake up and find
	a lemon strangled inside each fist
What do you call it	when a body choked by terror
	becomes the softest thing you hold

I call it hunger. I call it white cabbage. I call it flesh. I call it
throat sliced open by a tongue. I call it 人山人海. I call it belonging.
I call it sap-slick whiskey bottle. I call it flight. I call it swallow.
I call it pillowcase stuffed with bones. I call it egg yolk flicked on to
a sleeping face. I call it afterlife. I call it morning. I call it crows
ransacking an open surgery. I call it murder. I call it mother. I call it
slurping the gray juice out of a fish's eye. I call it bamboo stalks
in the backyard. I call it spit. I call it blue. I call it cello strings for
hair. I call it pulse. I call it suffer. I call it fight. I call it mine.

Say *Helli* & I will tell you where I came from. In Texas: a lottery ticket
drenched in honey emerges from my mother's thighs. My father takes
the ticket to the nearest gas station, fifteen miles north, where
the cashier hides a pistol in his boxer briefs: not knowing how
my father has sucked the gasoline out of a semi-truck. & somewhere
on the way home, the ticket is traded for a femur bone—
my mother scrapes it against the desert floor until she sees fire,
its flames curling into gingko leaves, reminding her of the city she
was born in, the city where smoke rises from everything:
soup dumplings, dragon-shaped rooftops, the skeletons of children
in the plaza. My mother & my father held hands before they walked
off the Nanjing Bridge. My mother & my father carried a box cutter
to slice a pathway through the ocean. My mother laced her breast milk
with peppercorn so her children could grow up to eat anything. &
from the desert fire, my mother dragged me out by my hair, birthing me.
Say *Hai Li* & I will stop pumping the trigger of this empty pistol. Say
my name & I will teach you how to leave your home behind
     & build a new one out of dust.

i've tried / to unwind the length of my shadow / across the field where we peeled our ankles to wipe our brows / a bare-throated finch trying to fill the desert clefs / with the hips of newspaper wads / & i have stood here for six sunfalls / scraping my mouth clean in the cold/ a lacecut membrane with beaded eyes / piking past a throatful of sand / as if made to douse these hours in wind / bodies surrendered to a loose boned fist / pulled inside another ill-fitted anatomy / where we swallow our bones like pythons & pray for our names to be called // so how are we supposed to kill a disease / if no one is there to watch it burn / through our lungs?

Wildfire
after Javier Zamora

Last summer I learned to walk
into an open mouth: white skylines caged
around my neck like a city on a leash.

I think of the way the boy spoke—as if
trying to swallow a plum—& realize
there is no easy way to say close. I've

fallen into cathedrals and landed on
my feet. I've strung and unstrung
a cello with my veins, still beating.

Because in the dark, what matters most
is how the shutter of a throat closes & not
how empty it is. I remember the night

I saw a woman's hips rise like a scaffold,
his hair on fire— the kind of fire that
shouts the need to be abandoned. So

I left. It's how I learned to walk away
they say. My sisters frozen in the field,
palms pressed against a corpse meant

to be mine. When the boy turned back,
I set the maple tree on fire. We watched
from the road. Two bodies split.

Topography of a Wound

I'll only say this once. My mother pinches
the seams of pork dumplings
as if she is afraid to hear them speak. My father spits out
pig feet bones like they are bullets.
In a Chinatown alley,
a skeleton falls to its knees inside its flesh
& shivers
like a wind-up toy in a plastic bag—

The last time I knelt for a man
was in an Applebee's parking lot. I cut a slit
in his belly, ate the guts & bones, and
placed a phoenix inside
just to see if it would fit.
When I visit my ancestors' graves
I leave a bouquet of trout spines
instead of lilies.

My mother's cabbage leaves
know how to choose their own colors
in the rain: the sobs of lightning
forcing us to look up at the sky. My mother
pinches the seams of pork dumplings
as if she is growing a garden of bruises.

& that night,
we stuck our hairdryers out the window
like silvered snipers
to try and talk back to the wind. How
the moonlight burned our flesh bright blue.
How we turned off all the lights in the house
& fell to our knees
just to hear the sound of bone.

Fallout

I woke up & it was dark. I woke up &
ate the dark. I woke up & carved
soup bowls from my collarbones. I woke
up & struck matches on my palms. I woke up
& drank the ashes from an urn. I
woke up & it was dark. It was dark & my
tongue walked out of my body. It was dark when
I knelt for prayer. It was dark & I tore pythons
out my wrists. It was dark & I woke up.
I woke up & all I saw was a burning hole
for where the window was meant to be.

Slow-Motion Suicide

It's the arrow you shot through
the bodies of two lovers

to try and pin them closer together.
It's the roadkill you carried home

in your mouth to learn the taste
of shock. It's the milk you tongued

from the kitchen tile & kissed back
into the carton, your mother outside,

beating the bamboo stalks
until they stood up straight. It's

the grave you filled with the
spooned-out heads of every man

who has traced a circle into
your thigh. It's each time you hear

nothing beats a quiet death
& it's what you say back: that in every field

soured by shotgun & bonemilk,
there is a house

with a door that leads to hell—

"No, vertigo is something other than the fear of falling. It is the voice of the emptiness below us which tempts and lures us, it is the desire to fall, against which, terrified, we defend ourselves."
Milan Kundera

When it is dark / I imagine the world is erasing my body / one bone at a time / like ashes / spreading in the river / When it is light / I pretend I can swallow sharks / twisters inside an open cage / My mother says / there is no use being alive / without a body / I say being alive / makes me want to burn / down a city / skeletons collapsed by light / clouds rushing ahead like / runaway trains / When I tried to die / the windows bared their teeth / because that night / our ancestors / escaped their lanterns / to remind us of the sky / how we see it as an ending / a mouth that never opens / so we left our incense sticks / in the cracks of the road / smoke rising / like a slow dance / between our steps / spines / hollowed into rain sticks / That is how we know / we are alone / everything burning / inside of us / like an old bookstore / trying to hold on / to everyone else's story / before its own / my father / sweeping the fruit basket / off the counter / to make room / for my mother's heaving body / slickened in moonlight / & in the old days / when we used to be alive / I sold my loose tooth / for a nickel / they say never hold on / to the things that try and escape you / It's how we learn / to fend for ourselves / a bird's body stiffened by wire / abandoned by its own flock / So, god / please tell me there are more / than five stages / of grief / tell me / there are people / who raise their fists / for something other / than war / like my mother / in the garden / scraping dew / with her knees / fists / knifed open / to touch the light / because I am tired / of cutting my hair / after every heartbreak / cutting my thighs / for every / opened vessel / because when the hurricane hit / my body swallowed everything / the fluency of water / the vacancy of glass / Here / I am tired / of being powerless

Haven't you heard? When your mother
lunges at you with a bread knife
it is only because she has
swallowed a hurricane for you,
her hair still swollen with salt &
tadpoles. And when you come home to
find your light bulbs replaced with moons,
know that it is just the Chinese
way of saying *please*. In the books
you are sky-colored & dressed in
doghide, smoke cloud bloomed by bullets.
If I could write, every door frame
we walked through would be shaped like
a girl. Your tongue catching bodies
the way we learn to hold chopsticks:
one pepper seed at a time. Don't
you know? The best place to bleed
out is in the snow. The man that
watches you sleep is just a boy
afraid of letting go. & if
you find your body spitting blue,
the way they drown crabs at the market,
think of the hands, damp & cherried
with rain, that once tore your mother
out of the house
she learned to dance in.

Pale Carnage

The more I am alive, the more I remember
how our bodies fell apart. As if someone spiralized
our bones and hung them as windchimes
above my bed. When it rains, the street tongue-slick
with color, I remember how you pressed your thumbs
into my throat— like you were trying to push something
out of me. I remember the way you cried, with all
the windows shut, your eyes sharpened into needles
to keep the light out. My name exits & re-exits a bathhouse
& you lick it out of my palm. *When tigers die,*
they leave behind their skins. Lately, I have been dressing myself
to look like the white bodies of fish in Chinese markets.
My own skin between layers of small teeth. *When humans die,*
they leave behind their names. When I die, I want to hear
the sound of a matchstick striking the sky & turning our breaths
into animals. When I die, this is what I will leave behind:
another mouth that won't open for the sake of hunger.

Entelechy

What makes it so easy
for a sewer to swallow

the last vestiges of rain
is impossible for my body

to understand. How we tear
apart from its surface, all

spark and religion, and tell
each other the same dream: still

crippled beneath the weight
of a penumbra, its blisters

loosened from bone, our
mothers scuttling at our heels

pinning our shadows
to telephone wires. A string

quartet wearing the city
's heartbeat learns the truth

of *limerence*: hands
scrape a ribcage open

to spill what is holy. We never
lose ourselves completely

but I lost a phoenix once,
in the mouth of a storm

and it gripped me with such
agony I forgot how

empty a body can feel
when its throat shuts down

like night: & before it flew
away I asked if it

was lonely and
it took my body and broke it

Somewhere: a house full of sewers learns to spit back out
Somewhere: a tank unzips a body, tooth by tooth
Somewhere: a deer eats the flowers off your mother's grave
Somewhere: I shot it dead
Somewhere: the Chinese word for *kneel*
Somewhere: a field that burns the color of flesh
Somewhere: shrapnel dissolving into birds
Somewhere: cockroaches bursting out of a shoe
Somewhere: your tongue pulling back a trigger
Somewhere: a skirt lifted to let in the wind
Somewhere: can't tell if it's smoke or rain
Somewhere: scotch-taped feathers to an airplane
Somewhere: a volcano swallowing down a song
Somewhere: your mother eating a bowl of cilantro
Somewhere: I held my breath so long the sky forgot me
Somewhere: carved daylight into a blade
Somewhere: a foot caught in the back of my throat
Somewhere: the ocean chewed into a tear
Somewhere:
      a fist full of sky, storm, & everything else left here to hold

Some days were made to be murmured.
A stranger spitting a yolk into your palm.
The wasp in the window curling into a clock.
Some stories were made to be kept.
So when they pillage your home
there's still something left to say in the dark.
A chandelier of birds & bones.
Some hands were made to feel cold.
So that when they touch you
your body knows to tear away faster.
Like the time I found your father's
whiskey bottle plugging up the bathtub.
Like the time we filled the vending machine with knives.
I've forgotten what I meant to say:
Only that a corpse, when robbed,
will teach itself to walk its way back home.

from the window of a stranger's house.
The wind beneath me like the strangled
echo of a firework. I wanted my body to move
so I tied a fishing net to each earlobe—

they caught nothing as I waited in the dark,
whiskeyed horizon laying a curtain
over our spines. & don't we touch ourselves
to remind us of the places where we are not

bruised? How the hollowed deer lying on the
windshield is just another corpse asking
to be carried home; how, from the inside
of a ribcage, it's harder to play the violin

in tune but easier to forget its geometry. Once
I watched as my mother crumpled to her knees
in the garage, her hair a halo of white smoke,
begging my father to run her body over. So I learned

what it means to lose restraint: that the sound
of someone else's heartbeat can splinter into
daylight if you replace it with your own. When
I looked back, I saw a man rushing towards me

in the night. His arms were open. I wanted to start
a fire in them. Because the body only remembers
what the mind wants to forget. & by the morning,
i found myself tossed into the river by a bridge

of hands, warm yet bloodlessly white.

Elegy for America
November 9, 2016

Instead, let it be how our mothers cupped
our skulls like limpets & poured our tears
down their throats—how we pressed finger
pistols to our spines and pretended our

bodies could grow wings—how, in winter,
even the earth loses itself to whiteness,
honeysuckle turning to bone, the bees shedding
their stripes like hair. & somewhere in

the city, a painted man learns to run with
more than his feet, the graveyard wolf-
whistling as he trips, ankles pinned down
by rain. The body remembers hope only after

it suffers the most. Behind the gate, a single
flame brightens my mother's face like a bomb
buried in snow. I touch her flesh & am reminded
of how she once passed through water to belong

here. Here: where I find a open clam in a room
full of fists. & somewhere in the city, a woman
weaves a veil out of her tongue—and all the tongues
left in the sewers that night—and destroys

her own body for a waiting man—

Leslie

When we opened the trunk, a naked man jumped out
and beat us with a crowbar. The car was an Aston M-
artin: but that's not what matters. What we saw on the
news is how that man screeched like a dog, his eyelids
pinned shut with forks, his cock nowhere to be found.
How we laughed through all the loose teeth & blood
rattling inside our mouths. Even the dragon asleep beneath the casino grinned into the collar of her *qipao*.
When we arrived home, we popped open beers on a
porch built over a grave, & watched another serial kill-
er hesitate before stabbing his taxi driver full of holes.

someone :   teach me what it means to survive
when I find myself   face-down   in a field
choked with white   as if waiting for some god
to carry me home   at times   I feed my legs
into railings &   beg the sky   to eat them off me
gravity   holding my hair upwards   to build
a black crown   teach me how to kneel   like
my mother   in the bathroom   razor moaning
against her scalp   a downpour of dark bullets
curled in her collarbones   how I almost mistook
the soft piano music   of her Korean drama
for a prayer   some might call it grief   I call
this forgetting   *ma ma:* teach me   what it means
to suffer quietly   how it must feel   to spit
without any teeth   the earth shaking the water
out of our palms   as if its sole purpose   was to
leave our bodies   empty   your coarse hair
small rivers   swollen with black fish   between
my toes   all I have learned   is how to starve

ABC Haibun

I was born in the room where my mother ate her first hamburger, the
room where my father sat at her bedside, licking every crumb off
her collarbone— the same room where, years later, we hung fish-shaped
lanterns on the smoke detectors, their bellies glowing the shape of bombs,
the room where the curtains held themselves open like a cut, the room
where my father learned that his body, when stripped, resembled the duck
he strangled & plucked in his youth, the room where he chain-smoked cigars
to remind himself how to breathe, his palms growing pockets
to hide the ashes, the room where my mother surrendered, face first, into
the bathtub, as if there was something in there to kiss, the room where
the TV told us that death is as frequent as rain, that rain mid-flight burns
just as much as when it lands, the room where I mistook my kneecaps
for the faces of my ancestors and prayed to them every night in the dark.

& I was born behind the counter of a laundry shop, where all the
towels we washed turned into stones, where the dryers learned how
to screech in Shanghainese and where my mother pressed cigarette
burns into all the white men's suits, despite the shudder of her hands,
where, when the men came back to beat her, the towels rose with their
butcher knives and scraped the men's tongues clean of spit, the lucky cat's
coin ripping a clean shot through the display window, and me, on my
knees behind the counter, sobbing all my teeth into the open mouth
of the cash register.

Plum peeled by bullets: all I asked
        was for my name / to be sung by wolves.

How to Peel a Sunflower Seed

As if undressing yourself
in the morning, skull split
open by a broken roof, the color

of bark around your thighs, the skirt
your mother sewed you pinned
to the walls, chopsticks burned in

the pit of your hair. As if
finally standing up after years of
crouching inside a bomb, your

spine curled like a clementine,
waiting to be pulled apart bone by
bone. As if thumbing open a lover

's mouth & finding a blood
ied carp for a tongue. Each tooth
a hollow lighthouse. My hands

learning how to murder you: as
if rescuing my own name,
& all its scattered bones,

out of a bur
                ning car—

Ignition

That was the last winter I let my body
learn to be lonely—two hands disguised as
the slackened jaw of my ribcage. Like how

dawn lights up but never burns the willow
paralyzed in the boneless field. From outside,
I watch my mother break open an egg:

her hands cradling the freckled shell with
such mercy, as if she could still hear it breathe,
before breaking the surface, a canary's glass eye

sobbing between her knuckles. How I wanted
my body to open that way. As if everything
left to swallow in this world was already

inside of me, waiting to fill some stranger's
half-open palm. Two strangers lying facedown
in a garden ask about danger, their mouths full

of milkweed. *Why is it that the more we touch
each other the smaller we feel?* Maybe
the only thing we were meant to taste is the breath

of our own prayers. Not the curtain of rain falling
from our cheekbones, not the seed-shaped
whiskey stain on the bedsheets, not the orange peel

pulled taut against our teeth. Despite love—despite
suffering. Outside, a man lights a cigarette
with nothing but the burning antler of a deer.

I didn't watch him do it, but I believed it from
the way he smiled afterwards, tea-stained and loose,
as if there was nothing on earth more sweet

than the smoke rising from the body of another.

Pulse

Tell me he came from the body
& not from religion. Tell me
how the man inside the bullet

turned into a fist raised up against
the rain. How he walked into
the toothless mouth of the dance

floor just to watch another ribcage
unhinge into bleach-white petals.
I will never know what it means

to be afraid. As in compressing
a body into a bruise & praying
it will never be unclenched. As in

boxing a mouth into a sound-
proof oven, lungs scattering
into a crooked ellipsis. I am

watching this war outside a box
made of mirrors: when I dip my
hand inside, it comes back pebbled

with saltwater, as if swiped against
some stranger's jawline in need
of another person's warmth.

In the sky, there are white vultures
circling a blood-lipped cathedral.

My mother's ponytail

moves as if
it had just won
a gunfight, head bowed
to enter the police car,
the minefield behind them
plugged up with bodies.
Afterwards, in the kitchen,
I dress each wound
with dumpling skins,
dipping them into the sea
to glue the ends shut. My
mother's ponytail
is the curtain
a man steps through
to meet his new bride,
only to find
the corpse of a dress
& a dollar bill, it is
the skinned soldier
slapping the blood
out of his ears, before
climbing out of the well
they threw him in; it is
the bodies of students
in Tiananmen Square
rolled into egg noodles
beneath the wheels
of army tanks. When we cut
my mother's hair off,
the ponytail stayed
tied together. I tossed it
into our fish tank
to watch it dance.
Even then, I could still
taste its scent
of diced bittermelon,
of our plastic bonsai tree
in flames, of
          a pulse
slowing beneath the sun.

Village of Knives

I say go back to where you came from.
In Hangzhou, where you washed your face
in a storm drain, your body pressed to the road

like a scab. Where you lit your father's
cigarette by running into a burning building.
Your father's fingers around your throat,

kneading a pulse back into you. Where
you once watched a girl steal a jackfruit
by clenching it between her thighs. Where

you tried to do the same, and walked home
with blood filling your shoes. I say
swallow what you can't keep. So when

your uncle tells you that red is the color
of China, show him your hands, how
you sharpened a sword on them

every morning before walking out the door.
& when your mother praises you
for eating every grain of rice, tell her

how you swallowed your fingernails
trying to stab the ghosts inside
of you. I say the ocean is the only thing

that knows how to forget. & so I spill over
every shopping cart full of mooncakes,
peel the mothers from their dragon-print

dresses, wring the piss out of every child
squatting in their backyard, & hurl it all off
the interstate bridge

       to learn the sound of drowning.

Self-Portrait as Postmortem

If you listen closely, you can hear gravity
          parting its thighs. My own name a metronome

beneath the tongue. This story goes: once I let a boy
          cut my stomach open with an earring

and slip inside like a sleeping bag. Once I lured a rabbit
          with my palm & bit its head clean off.

For months, I've tried to birth my own ocean,
          a place where they call murder

a miracle of nature. Because somewhere
          beneath these floorboards lives

the body of my body: the one I sobbed into
          tumbleweed: the one where my prayers took refuge

until it broke from the inside out. At night, I look down
          from jagged rooftops and watch the windows

close their eyes. It is like a ghost remembering
          bone— how it feels to swallow & be swallowed

all at once, a burning honeycomb spitting bees,
          each stinger lit to resemble a wound. How I want to eat

every beam of light that passes through me,
          like some fire-sucking god, dismantling every blade

too sharp to live inside of us—

Hey, Helli. I wanted to start this interview off by diving into the wonderful title of your chapbook, *Village of Knives.* **There is a constant push-and-pull in these poems between a communal "village" of heritage/traditions and the truly intimate investigations into your own life, into how the "knives" pierce you specifically. When you set out to write these poems, were your concerns initially more communal or personal? What changed as this collection started to form?**

In the past, I only ever wrote poems that were deeply personal to my own life. Even if the poems were concerned with larger events or ideas, I would always refer back to myself in writing about them. However, in the past few years, in my search for my own identity and sense of self as a poet, I've been reading as many works written by Asian American writers as possible. In doing this, I think my poems have naturally opened up to embrace a more communal space. Although writing about my personal life is still a huge part of my poetry, I think there is a sense of generosity and solidarity that comes with writing collectively—an extended hand towards the reader to let them know that I am thinking, writing, and feeling this, too.

At *Driftwood Press,* **we read a lot of poems that address parents and how the poet was raised, but very few reach your poems' levels of honesty and transparency. You write, "I watched as my mother crumpled to her knees / in the garage, her hair a halo of white smoke, / begging my father to run her body over." Was your relationship to your mother something you intentionally set out to write about or did it appear as you wrote? What were the hardest and easiest parts of writing about family?**

I write with conscious intention about family—like many children of immigrants or refugees, I feel a deep desire to voice my family's stories and experiences, ones that would otherwise largely be left unheard. For me personally, I think the hardest part of writing about family is telling the truth. My parents rarely share any details of their experiences as immigrants in America or about their lives back in China. And, even if they did, I still feel like I wouldn't be able to truly understand what they had gone through, how they had felt. So I often find myself filling in these gaps by crafting my own versions of their stories. That image you quoted may or may not have truly happened, but either way, I wrote it because I wanted to embody the immense hurt and loneliness that my parents faced. And it's that emotion that I'm trying my hardest to stay truthful to.

This is something I am always fascinated by, the different definitions of truth in writing, because I think every poet handles it differently. Mary Oliver wants us to know that the hawks and trees and shorelines are a beautiful and tangible fact, whereas someone like Anne Carson forces us into the unseen corners of our lives. Is truth at the forefront when you are drafting a poem? How important are facts to your writing?

In terms of facts, I think that I deliberately stray from incorporating a lot of objective truths in my poems, especially when re-imagining and rewriting real-life histories and experiences. I could have written journalistic essays or historical accounts about these same experiences, but I feel that I'm personally able to more poignantly convey them through poetry, where I can dream of images, characters, and worlds wildly beyond the scope of a purely factual or informative portrayal. Because I can explore parts of these experiences I wouldn't be able to access through other forms, I think that this approach can still be defined as "truth." That's the beauty of poetry, at least for me—having the freedom to erase the harsh boundaries that surround certain events, and being able to approach them on more subjective and interpretative terms.

Nearly every poem in *Village of Knives* is home to some kind of body imagery, often with a grotesque or mystical bend. Similar to some of Sharon Olds' most arresting work, these descriptions portray the body as both shelter and storehouse, a thing to hide in and, simultaneously, a thing that can be emptied. In your own experience, what do poets gain by morphing and manipulating a physical body in a poem? What could be lost?

I'm really fascinated by the physical body, and even more so by the grotesque. I think that the body, which is something that feels simultaneously incredibly familiar and incredibly unfamiliar to me, is a crucial part of my own poetry. I love poems that are shocking, and, to me, it feels like distorting the body is the most intimate and vulnerable way to turn heads in a poem. In addition, I have been thinking a lot lately about the importance of being explicit in writing about the violence and trauma of minority bodies. Poems that are brutally candid are the ones that stay with me the most, such as the language in Emily Jungmin Yoon's *A Cruelty Special to Our Species*. And I think this effect is necessary in making these often misrepresented and unheard traumas known, and even more importantly, remembered. In writing about my parents' traumas as well as my own, not only am I writing towards my own emotions and feelings, but I am also attempting to bring these difficult stories of immigrants and refugees to visible light.

One of my favorite things about this collection is the subtle visual experimentation. Ampersands, backslashes, word repetition and embedded spacing. When viewed together, these visual choices add layers of texture and three-dimensionality to poems already brimming with suspense and emotion. Did these stylistic choices appear in your first drafts, or were they elements you added in revision? In your own words, what are the strengths of utilizing more experimental formatting in a poem?

One of my favorite poets, Ocean Vuong, often uses ampersands in his poems. One of his poems, "My Father Writes From Prison," begins: "Lan oi, / Em khỏe khong? Giờ em đang ở đâu? Anh nhờ em va con qua. Hơn nữa & there are things / I can say only in the dark…" I'm particularly interested in the universality of the visual aspects of language, especially in poetry, and how the way a poem looks carries just as much weight as what it says. To me, the use of the ampersand in "My Father Writes From Prison" is incredibly powerful in that it appears on the page as a symbolic bridge between the two languages of Vietnamese and English— something that wouldn't exist if Vuong had simply written out the word "and." It's such a small moment in the poem, but I feel that it speaks so much to the boundaries of language and the Asian American identity. The & is so beautiful to me in that way. I feel similarly about other visual elements in poetry such as spacing, slashes, em dashes, asterisks, lack of capitalization, etc.

How long had you been working on this collection? What poems, structures, or ideas didn't make it into the final manuscript, and why were they cut?

Village of Knives is a collection of around four to five years' worth of poems, a few of which I even wrote (in their first forms) in high school. I think only recently, probably in the last year, did I come to a closer understanding of what themes and images really interest me as a writer, and that point is when I had to make enormous cuts and revisions to the manuscript.

As a reader, I think one of the most fascinating parts about a finished collection of poems is the sense of intrinsic finality in it; for *Village of Knives* specifically, it is great to see the cultural and personal concerns reach a fever pitch, even in a

smaller chapbook setting. What's equally fascinating, however, is whether or not the poet also senses this finality. Do you think you will return to the concerns of *Village of Knives* in future poems? What, if any, aspects of *Village of Knives* feel complete or finished for you as a poet?

While there are aspects to *Village of Knives* that I think will always stay in my poems in some form—family, heritage, trauma—there are several aspects that I do feel content to leave behind. I think that I tend to write within a set of recurring themes and images that cycle around each other within this collection, and moving forward, I feel very ready to lay those particular images to rest and explore my interests within a new perspective. Moving forward, I'm especially excited to experiment with forms I've never attempted to write before, such as prose poems, longer sequence poems, and structural forms such as villanelles and sestinas.

More to that above point, what is next for Helli Fang? Simply, what are you working on right now, and how might it differ from *Village of Knives*?

I'm currently a senior at Bard College and am working on my literature thesis exploring intergenerational and inherited trauma in Asian American poetry. I'm writing a collection of poems alongside this thesis, which consists of a sequence of prose poems that illustrate scenes of personal trauma, historical trauma, and family trauma. I'm hoping to continue this work after I graduate and hopefully publish them as a full-length collection.

> **The above interview with Helli Fang was conducted via email by Jerrod Schwarz.**

Helli Fang is an undergraduate student at Bard College. Her poetry has appeared or is forthcoming in *Diode, The Margins, Salt Hill, The Adroit Journal, DIALOGIST, Columbia Journal, Blueshift Journal, Wildness*, and more, and has been recognized by the Scholastic Art & Writing Awards, Columbia College of Chicago, and Bennington College. She has also participated in programs such as Iowa Young Writer's Workshop, The Adroit Mentorship Program, and The Speakeasy Project. Currently, she works as the communications intern for Kundiman. When Helli is not writing, she enjoys playing the violin and climbing trees.

Thank you to the editors of the following publications for featuring poems from this collection, often in different forms:

"ars poetica" *Alexandria Quarterly*, 2017.
"Genesis" & "Name:" *Diode*, 2019.
"The Waiting Room" *Wildness*, 2016.
"Wildfire," "Pulse" *Adroit Journal*, 2017.
"Aftershock" *DIALOGIST*, 2017.
"Obituary in Red Envelope" *The Margins*, 2019.
"Pale Carnage" *Salt Hill Journal*, 2018.
"Entelechy" *Souvenir Lit*, 2016.
"Last night I watched myself turn red" *Moledro Magazine*, 2017.
"Elegy for America" *States of the Union*, 2018.
"Ignition" *Blueshift Journal*, 2017.
"Self-Portrait as Postmortem" *Columbia Journal*, 2019.

Thank you to my teachers, Michael Ives, Robert Kelly, and Margaret Funkhouser, for your endless generosity, faith, and guidance, and for helping me find the courage to write. Thank you to my Kundiman family, to Chen Chen, and to the editors at *Driftwood*. Thank you to Lilly, for your quiet but unwavering love and support. To Mom & Dad, thank you for all that you've given me. My poems will always be for you.

CPSIA information can be obtained
at www.ICGtesting.com
Printed in the USA
JSHW020423270120
3818JS00004B/16

9 781949 065060